POND
LIFE

Text/Consultant: Terence Lindsey
Illustrator: Simone End

Published by
The National Geographic Society
Reg Murphy, President and Chief Executive Officer
Gilbert M. Grosvenor, Chairman of the Board
Nina D. Hoffman, Senior Vice President
William R. Gray, Vice President and Director, Book Division
Barbara Lalicki, Director of Children's Publishing
Barbara Brownell, Senior Editor
Mark A. Caraluzzi, Marketing Manager
Vincent P. Ryan, Manufacturing Manager

Library of Congress Catalog Number: 96-068854
ISBN: 0-7922-3449-9

Produced for the National Geographic Society by Weldon Owen Pty Ltd
43 Victoria Street, McMahons Point, NSW 2060, Australia
A member of the Weldon Owen Group of Companies
Sydney • San Francisco

President: John Owen
Publisher: Sheena Coupe
Project Editor: Jenni Bruce
Text Editor: Robert Coupe
Assistant Editor: Elizabeth Connolly
Art Director: Sue Burk
Designer: Mark Thacker
Photo Researcher: Amanda Weir
Production Manager: Caroline Webber

Film production by Mandarin Offset
Printed in Mexico

**MY FIRST
POCKET
GUIDE**

POND
LIFE

TERENCE LINDSEY

**NATIONAL
GEOGRAPHIC
SOCIETY**

INTRODUCTION

When rain falls, some soaks into the ground, but the rest usually drains away, flowing downhill to form a river or a stream. Sometimes rain falls in a flat place where it cannot flow away easily. The place is called a pond if it is small, and a lake if it is large. If it is filled with plants and grasses, it is called a marsh. If lots of trees grow in the place, it is called a swamp. All of these places are wetlands. They have fresh water, not salty water like the sea.

Animals of many kinds live in ponds and other wetlands. Some, such as fish, stay in the water all their lives. Others, such as dragonflies and frogs, live out of the water when they become adults.

You can catch many of these animals with a small net on a long stick. Put them in a jar of water to look at them closely, but always return them to their pond. Be careful when you handle pond creatures—some have a painful bite!

HOW TO USE THIS BOOK

This book is organized by type of animal. First come invertebrates, or animals without backbones—such as snails, insects, and crayfish. They are followed on page 38 by vertebrates, or animals with backbones— fish, reptiles, amphibians, birds, and mammals. Each spread helps you to identify one kind of pond animal. It tells you about the animal's color, appearance, behavior, and size. Use the ruler on the inside back cover to check how long it is. Animals that are very tiny are enlarged in the pictures. A shaded map of North America shows where to find the animal, and you can discover an unusual fact in the "Field Notes." If you come across a word you do not know, look it up in the Glossary on page 76.

HYDRA

 A hydra is a small, jellylike creature with five to seven long tentacles. Inside its tentacles, it has fine threads that shoot out to harpoon tiny animals. A poison dart on the tip of each thread paralyzes the prey.

WHERE TO FIND:
Hydras live among water plants in ponds, marshes, and slow streams throughout most of North America.

WHAT TO LOOK FOR:

✳ SIZE
A hydra grows to about one inch long.

✳ COLOR
Most hydras are green or yellowish.

✳ BEHAVIOR
Sometimes a hydra will drift in the water, but it mainly stays anchored to a water plant, waving its tentacles about. Several hydras may cluster together.

✳ MORE
A hydra usually begins life as a bud that grows on another hydra, then breaks off.

Hydras usually have their tentacles extended, but if you touch them, they will suddenly pull them in.

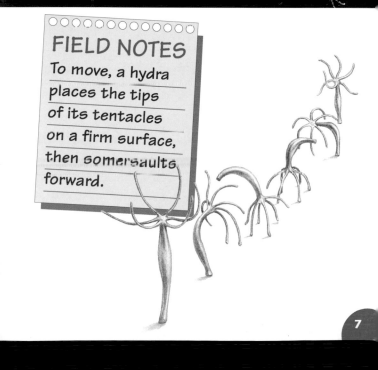

FIELD NOTES

To move, a hydra places the tips of its tentacles on a firm surface, then somersaults forward.

LEECH

 A leech can stretch out to be long and thin, or scrunch up to be small and fat. There's a sucker at each end of its wormlike body. The leech uses this to attach itself to fish and other prey and suck out their blood for food.

FIELD NOTES
Doctors once tried to cure sick patients by "bleeding" them with leeches.

A leech swims by rippling its body up and down.

Mussels live in freshwater ponds, marshes, streams, and rivers in most parts of North America.

WHAT TO LOOK FOR:

✳ SIZE
The widest part of a mussel's shell measures two to four inches across.

✳ COLOR
The shell is blackish or dark brown.

✳ BEHAVIOR
Until they are big enough to live on the bottom of their pond, baby mussels live in the fins and gills of fish.

✳ MORE
Once they settle on the bottom, mussels almost never move around again.

POND SNAIL

Although a pond snail can stay underwater for several hours, it usually comes to the surface every few minutes to breathe air. It has a breathing hole in its skin that closes when it goes back underwater.

The spiral shell of a pond snail ends in a sharp point called a spire.

WHERE TO FIND:
Pond snails live in ponds, lakes, and streams in the northeastern United States and across Canada.

WHAT TO LOOK FOR:

✳ **SIZE**
A pond snail's shell is about two inches long—about as long as your first finger.

✳ **COLOR**
The shells of most pond snails are pale brown or dull pink.

✳ **BEHAVIOR**
If you disturb a pond snail, it will pull its body back into its shell.

✳ **MORE**
A pond snail uses its rough tongue to scrape algae (AL-gee) off water plants.

FIELD NOTES
A pond snail lays its eggs in long, ropelike masses on the surface of the water.

WATER FLEA

 A single pond can contain millions of water fleas. These tiny creatures are often eaten by fish. All water fleas have four antennae (an-TEN-ee)—two for sensing danger, and two for rowing through the water.

WHERE TO FIND:
Water fleas live in most ponds. To see them, dip a glass into shallow water and hold it up to the light.

WHAT TO LOOK FOR:

✳ **SIZE**
Water fleas are less than one-tenth of an inch long—about as big as a sand grain.

✳ **COLOR**
They are usually see-through, but some are slightly brownish.

✳ **BEHAVIOR**
They move through the water with tiny, jerky movements.

✳ **MORE**
A water flea has one main eye. It is small and black.

A water flea has a pair of antennae on each side of its head.

FIELD NOTES
With a magnifying glass, you may see a female water flea's eggs in a pouch on her back.

FRESHWATER CRAYFISH

Crayfish usually spend the day in a burrow or under a stone, and come out at night to hunt for snails, insects, and tadpoles. You might see their cast-off shells floating in the water.

FIELD NOTES
When it grows too big for its shell, a crayfish sheds it. Its skin soon hardens into a new shell.

A crayfish has long antennae. Its eyes are on two short stalks.

WHERE TO FIND:
Crayfish are widespread. Look in ponds and streams that have hiding places such as rocks or muddy banks.

WHAT TO LOOK FOR:

✳ SIZE
Most crayfish grow between two and four inches long.

✳ COLOR
They are usually grayish or dark brown, but they can be bright blue or orange.

✳ BEHAVIOR
When disturbed, a crayfish will suddenly swim away backward. It does this by jerking its tail forward beneath its body.

✳ MORE
A crayfish has two large claws.

FISHING SPIDER

 A mother fishing spider carries her eggs around with her, then spins a web, puts the eggs inside, and stands guard until they hatch. This is why fishing spiders are also called nursery-web spiders.

WHERE TO FIND:
Look among water plants on the banks of ponds, marshes, and streams throughout most of North America.

WHAT TO LOOK FOR:

✻ SIZE
A fishing spider's body is about an inch long. With legs outstretched, the spider can be three or four inches wide.

✻ COLOR
It is usually a dull grayish brown.

✻ BEHAVIOR
A fishing spider finds its prey by sensing tiny ripples in the water with the tips of its front legs.

✻ MORE
It hunts mostly during the day.

18

A fishing spider has eight eyes, arranged in two rows across its face.

FIELD NOTES

When a fishing spider senses the movement of its prey underwater, it will dive to catch it.

19

DRAGONFLY

As a dragonfly flies quickly past you, listen for the dry, rustling sound made by its wings. Dragonflies can spend hours "on patrol," looking for small insects, such as flies and mosquitoes, to eat.

FIELD NOTES

Before a dragonfly becomes an adult, it lives underwater and is called a nymph. It often hunts small fish.

A young dragonfly, just out of the water, rests on a stem until its wings harden.

WHERE TO FIND:
You will find dragonflies in ponds, marshes, and quiet streams across almost all of North America.

WHAT TO LOOK FOR:

✳ SIZE
Dragonflies usually grow between one and four inches long.

✳ COLOR
They have bright blue, green, or red bodies, and see-through wings.

✳ BEHAVIOR
Some fly around all day long. Others wait on reed stems for insects to pass by.

✳ MORE
They have long, slender bodies and huge eyes.

GIANT WATER BUG

 If you pick up a giant water bug it will probably "play dead," but it might suddenly stab you with its sharp beak. The bug can use its beak to inject poison into its prey of water insects, tadpoles, and tiny fish.

WHERE TO FIND:
Giant water bugs live across most of North America. Look for them among water plants in shallow ponds.

WHAT TO LOOK FOR:

✳ SIZE
They can grow to more than two inches, but most are about an inch long.

✳ COLOR
They are usually dark brown.

✳ BEHAVIOR
At night, they often fly near lights. Some people call them "electric light bugs."

✳ MORE
When it is not flying, a giant water bug folds its see-through back wings under its hard, shell-like front wings.

Most giant water bugs
live alone. When two
of them meet, they are
likely to fight.

FIELD NOTES

The female water
bug often lays
her eggs on the
male's back, where
they stay until
they hatch.

WATER BOATMAN

The back legs of water boatmen are long and flattened like oars. A water boatman uses its back legs to row through the water, while its front legs collect tiny bits of plants to eat.

Stiff hairs, like the teeth of a comb, fringe a water boatman's back legs.

WHERE TO FIND:
They prefer shallow ponds, but are common in all kinds of wetlands where water plants grow.

WHAT TO LOOK FOR:

✳ SIZE
A water boatman grows about half an inch long.

✳ COLOR
It is usually dark gray or brownish.

✳ BEHAVIOR
As a water boatman swims underwater, it often zigzags on its course.

✳ MORE
Water boatmen fly from one pond to another in search of food. They often land in birdbaths.

FIELD NOTES
When a water boatman dives, it carries one or two air bubbles so that it can breathe.

25

BACK SWIMMER

Clinging to a water plant, a back swimmer waits underwater for tadpoles and small fish to swim above it. When they do, it lets go, drifts upward, and snatches its prey.

They are called back swimmers because they swim belly up, rowing with their back legs.

WHERE TO FIND:
You will see back swimmers in ponds, marshes, swamps, and rivers in almost all parts of North America.

WHAT TO LOOK FOR:

✳ **SIZE**
Back swimmers grow between a quarter- and a half-inch long.

✳ **COLOR**
Many are dull brownish or greenish, but some have brightly colored patterns.

✳ **BEHAVIOR**
Males attract females by rubbing their front legs noisily against their beaks.

✳ **MORE**
They sometimes bite people. Their bite feels like a bee sting.

WATER STRIDER

 If a small insect falls into a pond or stream, you may see a water strider skate over on long, outspread legs to eat it. Water striders hardly ever leave the surface of the water.

WHERE TO FIND:
You can see them in all kinds of wetlands across most of North America. Some even live on the ocean.

WHAT TO LOOK FOR:

✳ SIZE
A water strider's body is between a quarter- and a half-inch long.

✳ COLOR
Most kinds are blackish or dull brown.

✳ BEHAVIOR
Water striders usually move about in packs. You seldom see one by itself.

✳ MORE
If a strider gets its feet wet, it must crawl out of the water until they dry. Otherwise it would sink.

Only the tips of a water strider's legs touch the water. Its feet are farther up on its legs.

DIVING BEETLE

When it dives underwater, a diving beetle breathes from a bubble of air in a chamber under its wings. It has two pairs of wings—the pair it uses for flying are beneath its hard, outer wings.

When they are not swimming, diving beetles rest by holding onto plants.

WHERE TO FIND:
Diving beetles live across much of North America in ponds and streams where water plants grow thickly.

WHAT TO LOOK FOR:

✳ SIZE
Diving beetles grow about an inch long.

✳ COLOR
They are glossy black, with dull yellow markings on their heads and backs, and yellow on the edges of their front wings.

✳ BEHAVIOR
In winter, they stay buried in mud on the bottom of ponds.

✳ MORE
Diving beetles sometimes fly from one pond to another at night.

FIELD NOTES
Diving beetle larvae (LAR-vee) are often called water tigers. They are fierce hunters of small pond animals.

WHIRLIGIG BEETLE

All through winter, whirligig beetles lie buried in the mud at the bottom of ponds and lakes. In spring, they come to the surface to lay their eggs. They get their name from their habit of spinning rapidly in endless circles.

FIELD NOTES

You seldom see a whirligig beetle alone. They usually gather into large, quickly moving masses.

WHERE TO FIND:

Whirligigs are found in most of North America. Look for them moving in circles on ponds and slow streams.

WHAT TO LOOK FOR:

✳ SIZE
Whirligigs are about half an inch long.

✳ COLOR
They are shiny black.

✳ BEHAVIOR
Although most at home spinning on the surface of the water, whirligigs can also dive and fly.

✳ MORE
They use their short back legs, which are hidden beneath their bodies, to paddle around on the water.

A whirligig beetle has two pairs of eyes. The pair on top of its head sees clearly in air. The bottom pair sees well underwater.

MOSQUITO

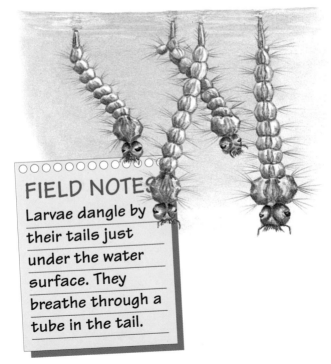

When it flies, a mosquito (muh-SKEET-oh) beats its wings so quickly that they make a high-pitched, whining noise. Female mosquitoes bite people or animals. The blood they suck out helps their eggs to hatch properly.

FIELD NOTES

Larvae dangle by their tails just under the water surface. They breathe through a tube in the tail.

Male mosquitoes, like this one, have very feathery antennae. Females' are less hairy.

WHERE TO FIND:
You will find mosquitoes, or they will find you, almost anywhere near still water such as ponds and marshes.

WHAT TO LOOK FOR:

✳ SIZE
Most are about a quarter-inch long.

✳ COLOR
They are dull brown.

✳ BEHAVIOR
Both males and females feed mainly on plant juices. Females pierce the skin of animals with a long tube called a proboscis (pruh-BAH-suhs).

✳ MORE
Larvae are often called wrigglers. They feed mostly on algae (AL-gee).

CADDIS FLY

Some caddis fly larvae live underwater in shelters that they build from tiny pebbles or twigs. When they are ready to turn into adults, they seal themselves into these shelters. Finally, as adults, they bite their way out and swim to the surface.

FIELD NOTES

When they move around underwater, caddis fly larvae always carry their shelters with them.

WHERE TO FIND:
Caddis fly larvae live in ponds and quiet streams across North America. The adults lay their eggs in water.

WHAT TO LOOK FOR:

✳ **SIZE**
Adult caddis flies vary in size, but they can grow to about an inch long.

✳ **COLOR**
Adults and larvae are usually brownish.

✳ **BEHAVIOR**
Adult caddis flies are attracted to street lights. They can look a bit like moths.

✳ **MORE**
Larvae can take up to a year to turn into adults. Adults live only about a month. They both feed on plants.

Adult caddis flies usually fly at night. They spend the day resting in cool places.

FRESHWATER EEL

 When it is time to breed, eels leave their freshwater ponds and travel downstream to the sea. They swim into the middle of the Atlantic Ocean, where they mate, lay their eggs, and die.

WHERE TO FIND:
You can find eels in most ponds, lakes, marshes, and streams in eastern and central North America.

WHAT TO LOOK FOR:

✳ SIZE
A female eel can grow to three feet, but a male grows only about one foot long.

✳ COLOR
Eels have greenish black or gray backs and silvery white sides and bellies.

✳ BEHAVIOR
A female eel lays between 10 million and 20 million eggs.

✳ MORE
Newborn eels take about a year to swim to the fresh waters that their parents left.

Freshwater eels have large heads and long, snakelike bodies.

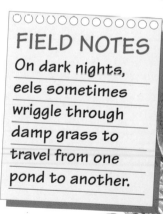

MINNOW

You cannot easily see the most unusual thing about a minnow. The teeth of this small fish are in its throat instead of in its mouth. Some kinds of minnows are called shiners because they look silvery.

FIELD NOTES

Minnows must always be ready for a quick escape. Many of their neighbors see them as food.

Unlike many other small fish, minnows have scales only on their bodies, not on their heads.

Minnows are common
in most North American
wetlands. They often
swim close to the shore.

WHAT TO LOOK FOR:

✳ SIZE
Most kinds of minnows grow between
two and six inches long.

✳ COLOR
Minnows are often golden with silvery
bellies. Some kinds are striped.

✳ BEHAVIOR
They eat algae and other water plants.

✳ MORE
In spring, male minnows grow little
lumps on their heads. These arc called
tubercles (TYOO-bur-kuhlz).

BULLHEAD CATFISH

 If its pond or stream dries up, a bullhead catfish can live for weeks buried in the mud on the bottom. When rain fills up its home again, the bullhead comes out to swim.

WHERE TO FIND:
Bullhead catfish live in muddy ponds and quiet streams, mainly in the United States and Mexico.

WHAT TO LOOK FOR:

✳ **SIZE**
Bullheads grow about one foot long.

✳ **COLOR**
They are mainly grayish or a blotchy yellowish color.

✳ **BEHAVIOR**
Females lay their eggs in nests on the muddy bottom. Males guard the young when they hatch.

✳ **MORE**
Their tails can be blunt and square or slightly rounded.

Most fish have scales on their skin, but catfish have smooth skin.

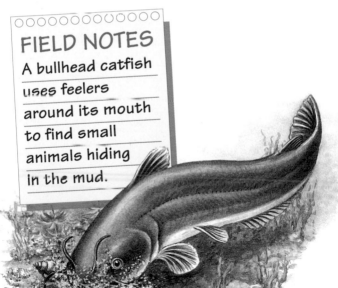

FIELD NOTES
A bullhead catfish uses feelers around its mouth to find small animals hiding in the mud.

BLUEGILL SUNFISH

In early spring, the male bluegill sunfish builds a nest of tiny pebbles on the bottom of its pond. The female visits the nest to lay as many as 50,000 eggs at a time.

A bluegill sunfish has a black spot on the gill cover behind each eye.

WHERE TO FIND:
Bluegill sunfish are common in ponds, shallow lakes, and quiet streams across much of North America.

WHAT TO LOOK FOR:

✳ SIZE
Adult bluegill sunfish are between six and nine inches long.

✳ COLOR
Bluegill sunfish vary in color, but most are greenish brown with paler sides and light grayish bars on their bodies.

✳ BEHAVIOR
They eat insects and small crayfish.

✳ MORE
The male bluegill sunfish guards the eggs in the nest until they hatch.

FIELD NOTES
In spring, the male's chest turns bright pink and his gill covers become light blue.

COMMON MUSK TURTLE

Except when it comes out to sunbathe on a floating log or up a sloping tree, a musk turtle stays in the water. You can often see one in a clear pond, swimming or walking slowly over the bottom and feeding on plants and small animals.

FIELD NOTES

A musk turtle can move its long neck and legs more easily than many other turtles can.

Green algae sometimes grow
on a musk turtle's shell.

WHERE TO FIND:
Musk turtles live mainly
in the eastern and central
United States, in still water
with a muddy bottom.

WHAT TO LOOK FOR:

✳ SIZE
A musk turtle is about as long as this
page is wide—about four inches.

✳ COLOR
It varies from dull brown to dark gray.
Algae can make its shell look greenish.

✳ BEHAVIOR
When frightened, musk turtles release
a smelly fluid from beneath their shells.
That's why they are also called stinkpots.

✳ MORE
A male musk turtle has a short, fat tail.

PAINTED TURTLE

Painted turtles are especially fond of ponds and lakes where the water is shallow, the bottom is muddy, and water plants grow thickly. In winter, they burrow into the oozy mud and go to sleep.

FIELD NOTES
The markings, especially on the underneath shell, vary depending on where they live.

WHERE TO FIND:
Look for them in ponds, marshes, and swamps in much of the United States and southern Canada.

WHAT TO LOOK FOR:

✳ SIZE
Painted turtles are about ten inches long.

✳ COLOR
They are mostly dark gray, with red and yellow markings on their heads and legs and on the rims of their shells.

✳ BEHAVIOR
A female lays between one and nine eggs in a scooped-out nest under a log.

✳ MORE
Painted turtles eat a wide range of food, from pondweed to frogs and fish.

Painted turtles often crawl onto logs.

49

COTTONMOUTH

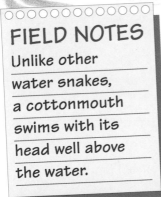

If a cottonmouth is disturbed, it may open its jaws to display the inside of its mouth, which looks as if it is lined with cotton. Stay away from this snake—its bite can kill a person. It often lies still when people come close.

FIELD NOTES

Unlike other water snakes, a cottonmouth swims with its head well above the water.

You can tell this is a young cottonmouth because its bands are clear and obvious.

WHAT TO LOOK FOR:

✳ SIZE
Cottonmouths can grow more than six feet long—as long as a man is tall.

✳ COLOR
They are usually dull brown with dark brown bands or blotches, but may turn completely dark when they get older.

✳ BEHAVIOR
When excited, they quiver their tails.

✳ MORE
At night, they hunt frogs, birds, and small mammals.

WATER SNAKE

 Quiet ponds and swamps are the favorite dwelling places of water snakes. You might also see them basking in the sun. In cool weather, they often burrow into piles of dead leaves.

WHERE TO FIND:
You can find water snakes in the eastern and central United States, in wetlands with lots of plants.

WHAT TO LOOK FOR:

✳ SIZE
Water snakes can grow six feet long.

✳ COLOR
They vary from green to black to dull red. Some have spotted patterns.

✳ BEHAVIOR
Many water snakes hunt during the day, but some are more active at night.

✳ MORE
If a water snake feels threatened, it often vomits up its last meal. It might also bite, but its bite is not poisonous.

There are many kinds of water snakes. This is a red-bellied water snake.

○○○○○○○○○○○○○○
FIELD NOTES
A water snake may dangle from a branch, waiting to pounce on fish.

MUD PUPPY

These salamanders are called mud puppies because people once thought they could bark like dogs—even though they can't. Mud puppies never leave the water. At night, they hunt small animals, such as snails.

FIELD NOTES
Mud puppies have blunt noses and paddle-shaped tails that help them to move through the water.

A mud puppy's gills are on the outside of its head. They are red and feathery.

WHERE TO FIND:
Mud puppies are hard to see, but you're most likely to find them in ponds and streams in central North America.

WHAT TO LOOK FOR:

✳ SIZE
A mud puppy can grow 17 inches long.

✳ COLOR
It may be gray, rusty brown, or nearly black, usually with dark spots.

✳ BEHAVIOR
A female mud puppy lays her eggs on the underside of a log or rock. She guards them for up to two months.

✳ MORE
A mud puppy has four feet. Each foot has four toes.

EASTERN NEWT

When newts first hatch, they live in water and breathe through gills. They lose their gills after a few months and move onto land. These land-dwellers are called efts. After several years, they become adults and return to the water.

FIELD NOTES
Efts have rounded tails, but adult newts, like this one, have tails that look flattened.

An eft is more colorful than an adult newt. It lives in mossy places.

WHERE TO FIND:
You can find newts in ponds and marshes, especially in woods, in eastern and central North America.

WHAT TO LOOK FOR:

✳ SIZE
An adult newt is about five inches long.

✳ COLOR
Adults are mostly dull green, often with bright red spots. They have yellow bellies with small black dots.

✳ BEHAVIOR
Newts eat small animals such as worms, insects, and tadpoles.

✳ MORE
Newts have poisonous skin, and this protects them against most enemies.

AMERICAN TOAD

During the day, American toads burrow in loose soil or hide in piles of dead leaves. At night, they come out to hunt, mainly for insects. In spring, they gather around ponds and marshes to breed.

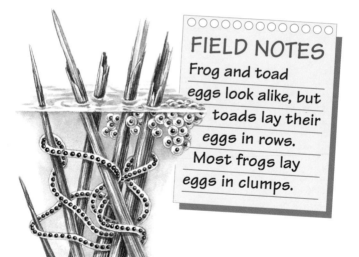

FIELD NOTES
Frog and toad eggs look alike, but toads lay their eggs in rows. Most frogs lay eggs in clumps.

A toad has dry, warty skin. It can squirt poison from behind its eyes at an attacker.

WHERE TO FIND:
The American toad lives in eastern and central North America, wherever there are lots of insects and moisture.

WHAT TO LOOK FOR:

✳ SIZE
Toads grow about four inches long—about as long as this page is wide.

✳ COLOR
They are usually dull brown or grayish, with blotches of darker brown.

✳ BEHAVIOR
An American toad's song is a trill that can last longer than 20 seconds.

✳ MORE
Toads shuffle and hop on short legs, but they do not jump like frogs.

CRICKET FROG

 Listen in spring for the noisy chorus of cricket frogs. Their song sounds like two pebbles being struck together, slowly at first, but then speeding up to a rapid trill of 20 to 30 clicks at a time.

WHERE TO FIND:
Look near ponds and streams in the eastern and central United States. They are active during the day.

WHAT TO LOOK FOR:

✳ SIZE
They are a little longer than an inch.

✳ COLOR
Most are green or brown, with darker brown bands or blotches.

✳ BEHAVIOR
Unlike most other frogs, female cricket frogs lay one egg at a time.

✳ MORE
If you go near them, they will probably jump into the water, but they may come out again on another part of the bank.

You can recognize a cricket frog by the triangle-shaped mark on its head.

FIELD NOTES
All baby frogs are called tadpoles. They look a bit like fish until their legs start to grow.

BULLFROG

Though it eats mainly insects and tadpoles, a bullfrog is big enough to catch small birds. Listen for its loud, deep call that sounds a bit like *jug-o-rum*. The bullfrog makes its call alone, and not in chorus.

A bullfrog's eyes are very high on its head. Its eardrums are behind its eyes.

WHAT TO LOOK FOR:

✳ SIZE
Bullfrogs grow about six inches long.

✳ COLOR
They are usually dull green, with brownish or grayish blotches on their backs and legs.

✳ BEHAVIOR
A bullfrog puffs up a pouch of skin under its chin to make its call louder.

✳ MORE
With their strong back legs, bullfrogs are long-distance jumpers.

FIELD NOTES
In spring, males often wrestle over females until one pushes the other onto its back and wins.

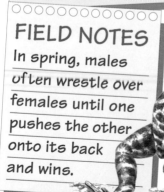

63

PIED-BILLED GREBE

 Pied-billed grebes often fly from pond to pond, but they almost never come ashore. They hunt fish and insects, and they also eat their own feathers. The feathers might protect their stomachs from sharp fish bones.

WHERE TO FIND:
They are common across most of North America. In winter, they travel to the warmer south.

WHAT TO LOOK FOR:

✳ **SIZE**
A pied-billed grebe measures about 14 inches.

✳ **COLOR**
It is brown with a black chin. Its bill is white with a black band and is called a pied bill because it has two colors.

✳ **BEHAVIOR**
If you disturb a grebe, it sinks in the water until only its head shows.

✳ **MORE**
In winter, its bill turns a dull yellow.

A grebe's tail is a mass of fluffy feathers, unlike the stiff feathers of most birds.

FIELD NOTES

Baby grebes often ride on their parents' backs, and may even stay there when the parent dives.

65

GREEN-BACKED HERON

This small, tubby bird stretches its neck out long and thin to stab small fish with its sharp bill. You might see one standing in shallow water and raking the bottom with its feet as it searches for fish.

FIELD NOTES

Green-backed herons go fishing! To attract fish, they drop leaves into the water as bait.

WHERE TO FIND:
In summer, look in wooded wetlands across much of North America. Many fly south to Mexico in winter.

WHAT TO LOOK FOR:

✳ SIZE
This heron grows about 18 inches long.

✳ COLOR
It is greenish gray on top with a black cap. Its breast, cheeks, and underparts are chestnut red.

✳ BEHAVIOR
If disturbed, this bird may flick its tail and raise shaggy feathers on its head.

✳ MORE
When males are courting, their legs turn from a yellowish to a deep orange color.

The green-backed heron is a quiet, shy bird and will often hide in thick cover.

WOOD DUCK

These birds are called wood ducks because they spend most of their time in ponds and streams deep in the woods. They live in pairs or family groups, and nest in holes high up in dead trees.

FIELD NOTES

Female wood ducks show their ducklings where to find food, but the ducklings must feed themselves.

Notice the male wood duck's green, purple, and white crest.

WHERE TO FIND:
Wood ducks live in parts of the United States, Canada, and Mexico. They fly south for winter.

WHAT TO LOOK FOR:

✳ SIZE
An adult wood duck is a little more than 18 inches long.

✳ COLOR
The male is brightly patterned, but the female is a dull brown.

✳ BEHAVIOR
Small flocks of wood ducks sometimes gather in winter. When they take flight, they often make a loud squealing sound.

✳ MORE
Wood ducks eat seeds and insects.

RED-WINGED BLACKBIRD

 If you look up at the sky in winter, you may see thousands of red-winged blackbirds flying south. They will return in spring to nest in pairs on the shores of wetlands.

WHERE TO FIND:
Red-winged blackbirds live throughout most of North America. In winter, many fly to the Southeast.

WHAT TO LOOK FOR:

✳ **SIZE**
They are almost nine inches long.

✳ **COLOR**
Adult males are glossy black all over, except for bright red patches on their shoulders. Females and young males are streaked with dark brown and white.

✳ **BEHAVIOR**
They feed mainly on the ground, eating insects, seeds, and berries.

✳ **MORE**
Their song sounds like *konk-a-ree*.

In spring, males sing loudly and display their shoulder patches to attract females.

FIELD NOTES

Females lay three to five spotted eggs. Their nests are often attached to reeds.

NORTHERN WATER SHREW

Except for their long, pointed noses and very tiny eyes, water shrews look a little like mice. Even though they are small, they are ferocious hunters and will even attack animals larger than themselves.

This water shrew is looking into a pond for a meal.

WHAT TO LOOK FOR:

✳ SIZE
A water shrew is just over six inches long, but three inches of this is its tail.

✳ COLOR
It is dark gray on top, and silvery or nearly white underneath.

✳ BEHAVIOR
When a shrew hunts, it uses hearing and sense of smell more than eyesight.

✳ MORE
Long, stiff hairs around a water shrew's back legs help it to swim.

FIELD NOTES

Water shrews hunt mostly in the water, and often dive when chasing insects, fish, or frogs.

MUSKRAT

Muskrats live in family groups in riverbank burrows or in houses called lodges that they build in shallow water. These mammals have thick fur all over, except on their tails, which are flat and scaly.

FIELD NOTES

Muskrats feed mainly on water plants, but they also hunt frogs, mussels, and small fish.

A muskrat family builds its lodge from mud and plant stalks.

WHERE TO FIND:
Muskrats live in ponds, lakes, marshes, and rivers throughout most of the United States and Canada.

WHAT TO LOOK FOR:

✳ SIZE
A muskrat measures about two feet from its nose to the tip of its tail.

✳ COLOR
Its fur is mainly dark brown or reddish brown. It is usually paler underneath.

✳ BEHAVIOR
It spends most of its time in the water.

✳ MORE
Muskrats are active all winter long, when you might see them running around on the ice of frozen ponds.

GLOSSARY

algae Plants that live in water and have no roots, leaves, or stems.

amphibian A cold-blooded animal, such as a frog or toad, that has moist skin without scales, and lays its eggs in water.

antennae Feelers on an animal's head that move around and pick up smells and vibrations from the air.

bask When an animal lies in the sun to soak up the warmth it needs to move around.

bill A bird's beak.

breed When adult males and females come together to produce young.

burrow A hole that an animal digs in the ground for its home.

crest Feathers that stand up on the heads of some birds.

gills The parts that underwater animals use for breathing.

larva The wormlike stage that comes between the egg and adult stages of insects.

mammal A warm-blooded animal, usually with hair or fur, that feeds its young on milk from the mother's body.

nymph The young, wingless stage that comes between the egg and adult stages of some insects.

paralyze To sting or poison prey so that it is still alive but cannot move.

prey Any animal hunted by other animals for food.

reptile A cold-blooded animal that has scaly or leathery skin and usually lays eggs. Snakes and turtles are reptiles.

tentacles The long, thin feelers that some animals use for grasping and feeding.

territory The place where an animal or a group of animals lives. Animals defend their territory from other animals of the same kind.

wetlands The general name for lakes, ponds, marshes, swamps, streams, and rivers.

INDEX OF
POND LIFE

ABOUT THE CONSULTANT

Terence Lindsey was born in England and raised and educated in Canada. He has traveled widely in North America, Europe, and Australasia, but has made Australia his home for the past 25 years. His interests encompass most of the natural world. He has studied, written, and taught mainly about birds, with a special interest in avian zoogeography and foraging and reproduction strategies. He is an Associate of the Australian Museum and a former tutor at the University of Sydney, but now devotes most of his time to writing, traveling, and consulting.

PHOTOGRAPHIC CREDITS